let's celebrate

thanksgiving

by J. Patrick Lewis

Children's Press®
An Imprint of Scholastic Inc.

Library of Congress Cataloging-in-Publication Data
A CIP catalog record for this book is available from the Library of Congress

Produced by Spooky Cheetah Press
Design by Anna Tunick Tabachnik (www.atunick.com)
Fonts: Coco Gothic, ITC Stone Informal
Clouds by freepik.com
Special thanks to Pamela Chanko for editorial advice

Printed in Heshan, China 62

SCHOLASTIC, CHILDREN'S PRESS, ROOKIE POETRY™, and associated logos are trademarks and/or registered trademarks of Scholastic Inc..

1 2 3 4 5 6 7 8 9 10 R 27 26 25 24 23 22 21 20 19 18

Scholastic Inc., 557 Broadway, New York, NY 10012.

table of contents

happy thanksgiving!

After rolling in leaves, we're ready to eat
Thanksgiving dinner on Happiness Street
with Grandma and Grandpa, our
   cousins and such.
So, stomachs, get ready—
   thank you so much!

FACT!
Thanksgiving
was officially
made a holiday
in 1863.

sharing
the first meal

Pilgrims and Native Americans
celebrated under the trees:
a **feast** that lasted three days—
and forever in our memories.

FACT!
The first feast included deer meat, duck, and corn.

oompa, boompa, boom-diddy-yay!

Here comes the holiday parade,
the big balloons and the marching band.
A giant turkey's on **display**.
Doesn't he look fat and grand?

FACT!
The Macy's
Thanksgiving Day
Parade began
in 1924.

the thank-you bird

The turkey is a wonderful bird,
who **struts** and gobbles all day.
But her **fondest** wish at Thanksgiving
is that she could run away!

FACT!
Each year, the president pardons one turkey.

tag football

Watch us run down the football field
as fast as we are able.
But, oh, that turkey smells so good—
we won't be late to the table.

FACT!
The first NFL
Thanksgiving game
was played
in 1934.

the feast

Pass the cornbread, pass the gravy,
sweet potatoes, save me a thigh.
I'm so stuffed I can't decide
if I've got room for pumpkin pie!

FACT!
Americans eat 46 million turkeys each Thanksgiving.

making wishes

Let's make a wish on the wishbone.
We can do it right after dinner.
We'll pull it and twist it and yank it...
 ccrraaack!
Looks like you're the winner!

FACT!
In England,
people call the
wishbone the
"merrythought."

a tomorrow sandwich

Thanksgiving dinner is over.
I'm sorry to go bed.
But tomorrow I'll eat all the leftovers
between two pieces of bread.

FACT!
In the U.S., about 49 million people travel for the holiday.

giving thanks around the world

Germany

A special crown
Germans give thanks with a harvest festival in October. Some people wear a crown made of flowers, grain, and fruit.

Liberia

Sweet offerings
Liberia was founded by freed American slaves. People here celebrate Thanksgiving by filling their churches with baskets of delicious local fruits.

The Netherlands

Church and cookies
In Leiden, a city in the Netherlands, they celebrate Thanksgiving with a church service followed by cookies and coffee.

China

Over the moon
For more than 3,000 years, people here have shown thanks for the changing seasons and the fall harvest. A favorite dessert for this thanksgiving celebration is moon cake: a pastry with a thick, sweet filling.

Grenada

For the troops
In 1983, U.S. troops helped restore peace on this island. The people threw a Thanksgiving feast to show their gratitude. They still celebrate an annual day of thanks.

Japan

Thanks, Officer
On November 23, people in Japan celebrate Labor Thanksgiving Day. This is a day to honor workers. Many children make gifts for local police officers.

21

thanksgiving is...

...a chance for people to show gratitude for their good fortune throughout the year. In the United States, we celebrate Thanksgiving on the fourth Thursday in November. People trace this tradition back to a celebration held almost 400 years ago.

In 1620, people we call Pilgrims left England to settle in America. Native Americans who lived in the area showed them how to survive in this new land. In the fall of 1621 the Pilgrims held a feast to celebrate their first successful harvest. They invited the Native Americans to join them. This became known as the first Thanksgiving.

Today, we celebrate Thanksgiving in different ways. Many people share a feast with family and friends. Some choose to spend the day helping others. No matter the celebration, Thanksgiving is a time for people to give thanks for all that is good in their lives.

glossary

display (dis-PLAY): Something that is shown or exhibited for the public.

feast (FEEST): A large, special meal, usually for a lot of people on a holiday or other occasion.

fondest (FAHND-est): Most liked or wished for.

Pilgrims (PIL-gruhms): The group of people who left England, came to America, and founded Plymouth Colony in 1620.

struts (STRUHTS): When someone or something walks in a proud way.

index

facts for now

Visit this Scholastic Web site to learn more about Thanksgiving:
www.factsfornow.scholastic.com Enter the keyword **Thanksgiving**

about the author

J. Patrick Lewis has published 100 children's picture and poetry books to date with a wide variety of publishers. The Poetry Foundation named him the third U.S. Children's Poet Laureate.